The Life Around Us

Books by Denise Levertov

DENISE LEVERTOV

The Life Around Us

SELECTED POEMS

ON NATURE

A New Directions Book

The Life Around Us incorporates poems from eleven previous Denise
Levertov books with New Directions: *The Sands of the Well* (1996), *Evening
Train* (1992), *A Door in the Hive* (1989), *Breathing the Water* (1987), *Oblique
Prayers* (1984), *Candles in Babylon* (1982), *Life in the Forest* (1978), *The
Freeing of the Dust* (1975), *Footprints* (1972), *The Sorrow Dance* (1966), and
The Jacob's Ladder (1961).

Designed by Sylvia Frezzolini Severance
Manufactured in the United States of America
New Directions Books are printed on acid-free paper
First published clothbound and as New Directions Paperbook 843 in 1997
Published simultaneously in Canada by Penguin Books Canada Limited

Library of Congress Cataloging in Publication Data

Levertov, Denise, 1923–
    The life around us : selected poems on ecological themes / Denise
Levertov
    p.   cm.
    ISBN 0-8112-1351-X (cloth : alk. paper). — ISBN 0-8112-1352-8
(pbk. : alk. paper)
    1. Ecology—Poetry.   I. Title
PS3562.E8876L48   1997
811'.54—dc21   96-52901
                                                                CIP

New Directions Books are published for James Laughlin
by New Directions Publishing Corporation
80 Eighth Avenue, New York 10011

Contents

Foreword

As I have quite frequently found myself obliged to skip back and forth from book to book when reading to audiences composed of people whose work and vocation was in ecology, conservation, and restoration, it was suggested that I put together a selection of thematically relevant poems, which would be useful not only to the many earth-science people who, I have found, do love poetry, but also to the general public.

In compiling this volume I've drawn mainly on my more recent books, but have included also a number of older poems, written when, like the rest of us, I was less conscious of all that threatens the earth, but nevertheless shared with most poets in every time and place an ardent love of what my eyes and other senses revealed to me in the world we call 'nature.'

In these last few decades of the twentieth century it has become ever clearer to all thinking people that although we humans are a part of nature ourselves, we have become, in multifarious ways, an increasingly destructive element within it, shaking and breaking the 'great web'—perhaps irremediably. So a poet, although often impelled, as always, to write poems of pure celebration, is driven inevitably to lament, to anger, and to the expression of dread. And in arranging the poems I've chosen here, I decided not to group them separately—praise-poems in one clump, laments and fears in another—but to follow (though not always in chronological order) the natural undulations and alternations I experienced in writing now in one vein, now in another, whether in separate poems or in those in which celebration and the fear of loss are necessarily conjoined. I believe this flux and reflux echo what readers also feel in their response to 'the green world.'

—Denise Levertov

The Life
Around Us

Often, it's nowhere special: maybe
a train rattling not fast or slow
from Melbourne to Sydney, and the light's fading,
we've passed that wide river remembered
from a tale about boyhood and fatal love, written
in vodka prose, clear and burning—
the light's fading and then
beside the tracks this particular
straggle of eucalypts, an inconsequential
bit of a wood, a coppice, looks your way,
not at you, through you, through the train,
over it—gazes with branches and rags of bark
to something beyond your passing. It's not,
this shred of seeing, more beautiful
than a million others, less so than many;
you have no past here, no memories,
and you'll never set foot among these shadowy
tentative presences. Perhaps when you've left this continent
you'll never return; but it stays with you:
years later, whenever
its blurry image flicks on in your head,
it wrenches from you the old cry:
O Earth, belovéd Earth!
                              —like many another faint
constellation of landscape does, or fragment
of lichened stone, or some old shed

where you took refuge once from pelting rain
in Essex, leaning on wheel or shafts
of a dusty cart, and came out when you heard
a blackbird return to song though the rain
was not quite over; and, as you thought there'd be,
there was, in the dark quarter where frowning clouds
were still clustered, a hesitant trace
of rainbow; and across from that the expected
gleam of East Anglian afternoon light, and leaves
dripping and shining. Puddles, and the roadside weeds
washed of their dust. Earth,
that inward cry again —
Erde, du liebe . . .

Animal willows of November
in pelt of gold enduring when all else
has let go all ornament
and stands naked in the cold.
Cold shine of sun on swamp water,
cold caress of slant beam on bough,
gray light on brown bark.
Willows—last to relinquish a leaf,
curious, patient, lion-headed, tense
with energy, watching
the serene cold through a curtain
of tarnished strands.

The cat on my bosom
sleeping and purring
—fur-petalled chrysanthemum,
squirrel-killer—

is a metaphor only if I
force him to be one,
looking too long in his pale, fond,
dilating, contracting eyes

that reject mirrors, refuse
to observe what bides
stockstill.
         Likewise

flex and reflex of claws
gently pricking through sweater to skin
gently sustain their own tune,
not mine. I-Thou, cat, I-Thou.

When to my melancholy
All is folly
            then the whirr
of the hummingbird
at intervals throughout the day

is all that's sure
to stir me, makes me
jump up, scattering

papers, books, pens—
                  To the bay window,
and certainly

there he is below it
true-aimed at the minute cups of
Coral Bells, swerving

perfectly,
the fierce, brilliant faith
that pierces the heart all summer

and sips bitter insects steeped in nectar,
prima materia
of gleam-and-speed-away.

A passion so intense
It driveth sorrow hence. . . .

Each day
the cardinals call and call in the rain,
each cadence scarlet
among leafless buckeye,

and passionately
the redbuds, that can't wait
like other blossoms, to flower
from fingertip twigs,
break forth

as Eve from Adam's
cage of ribs,
straight from amazed treetrunks.

Lumps of snow
are melting in tulip-cups.

The ash tree drops the few dry leaves it bore in May,
stands naked by mid-July.
When each day's evil news drains into the next,
a monotonous overflow,
has a tree's dying lost the right to be mourned?
No—life's indivisible. And this tree,
rooted beyond my fence, has been,
branch and curved twig, in leaf or bare, the net
that held the sky in my window.
Trunk in deep shade, its lofting crown
offers to each long day's
pale glow after the sun
is almost down, an answering gold—
the last light
held and caressed.

In their homes, much glass and steel. Their cars
are fast — walking's for children, except in rooms.
When they take longer trips, they think with contempt
of the jet's archaic slowness. Monastic
in dedication to work, they apply honed skills,
impatient of less than perfection. They sleep by day
when the bustle of lives might disturb their research,
and labor beneath fluorescent light in controlled environments
fitting their needs, as the dialects
in which they converse, with each other or with
the machines (which are not called machines)
are controlled and fitting. The air they breathe
is conditioned. Coffee and coke keep them alert.
But no one can say they don't dream,
that they have no vision. Their vision
consumes them, they think all the time
of the city in space, they long for the permanent colony,
not just a lab up there, the whole works,
malls, racquet courts, hot tubs, state-of-the-art
ski machines, entertainment . . . Imagine it, they think,
way out there, outside of 'nature,' unhampered,
a place contrived by man, supreme
triumph of reason. They know it will happen.
They do not love the earth.

The Wishing Well was a spring
bubbling clear and soundless into a shallow pool
less than three feet across, a hood of rocks
protecting it, smallest of grottoes, from falling leaves,
the pebbles of past wishes peacefully underwater, old desires
forgotten or fulfilled. No one threw money in, one had to search
for the right small stone.

This was the place from which
year after year in childhood I demanded my departure,
my journeying forth into the world of magical
cities, mountains, otherness—the place which gave
what I asked, and more; to which
still wandering, I returned this year, as if
to gaze once more at the face
of an ancient grandmother.
And I found the well
filled to the shallow brim
with debris of a culture's sickness—
with bottles, tins, paper, plastic—
the soiled bandages
of its aching unconsciousness.

Does the clogged spring still moisten
the underlayer of waste?
Was it children threw in the rubbish?

Children who don't dream, or dismiss
their own desires and
toss them down, discarded packaging?
I move away, walking fast, the impetus
of so many journeys pushes me on,
but where are the stricken children of this time, this place,
to travel to, in Time if not in Place,
the grandmother wellspring choked, and themselves not aware
of all they are doing-without?

The earth is the Lord's, we gabbled,
and the fullness thereof —
while we looted and pillaged, claiming indemnity:
the fullness thereof
given over to us, to our use —
while we preened ourselves, sure of our power,
wilful or ignorant, through the centuries.

Miswritten, misread, that charge:
subdue was the false, the misplaced word in the story.
Surely we were to have been
earth's mind, mirror, reflective source.
Surely our task
was to have been
to love the earth,
to *dress and keep it* like Eden's garden.

That would have been our *dominion:*
to be those cells of earth's body that could
perceive and imagine, could bring the planet
into the haven it is to be known,
(as the eye blesses the hand, perceiving
its form and the work it can do).

A man and woman
sit by the riverbank.
He fishes,
she reads.
The fish are not biting.
She has not turned the page
for an hour.
The light around them
holds itself taut,
no shadow moves,
but the sky and the woods,
look, are dark.
Night has advanced upon them.

Once a woman went into the woods.
The birds were silent. Why? she said.
Thunder, they told her,
thunder's coming.
She walked on, and the trees were dark
and rustled their leaves. Why? she said.
The great storm, they told her,
the great storm is coming.
She came to the river, it rushed by
without reply, she crossed the bridge,
she began to climb
up to the ridge where grey rocks
bleach themselves, waiting
for crack of doom,
and the hermit
had his hut, the wise man
who had lived since time began.
When she came to the hut
there was no one.
But she heard his axe.
She heard
the listening forest.
She dared not follow the sound
of the axe. Was it
the world-tree he was felling?
Was this the day?

The Vron Woods (*North Wales*)

In the night's dream of day
the woods were fragrant.
Carapaced, slender, vertical,
        red in the slant
        fragmented light, uprose
Scotch firs,
boughs a vague smoke of
green.
      Underfoot
             the slipping
of tawny needles.

I was wholly there,
aware of each step
in the hum of quietness,
each breath.
      Sunlight
a net
     of discs and lozenges, holding
odor of rosin.

These were the Vron Woods,

felled
seven years before I was born,

levelled,
to feed a war.

Intricate and untraceable
weaving and interweaving,
dark strand with light:

designed, beyond
all spiderly contrivance,
to link, not to entrap:

elation, grief, joy, contrition, entwined;
shaking, changing,
              forever
                   forming,
                         transforming:

all praise,
          all praise to the
                   great web.

The way the willow-bark
braids its furrows
is answered by the willow-branches
swaying their green leaf-weavings
over the river shallows,
assenting, affirming.

The mountain's spine, the cow's ridge,
the saddle dip,
                    high flanks,
spur of ranged
spruce, tail
to brush at flies, valley air
between them, and
                    nothing else.

It could be the râle of Earth's tight chest,
her lungs scarred from old fevers, and she asleep—

but there's no news from the seismographs,
the crystal pendant
hangs plumb from its hook;

and yet at times (and I whisper because
it's a fearful thing I tell you)
a subtle shudder has passed
from outside me into my bones,

up from the ground beneath me,
beneath this house, beneath
the road and the trees:

a silent delicate trembling no one has spoken of,
as if a beaten child or a captive animal
lay waiting the next blow.

It comes from the Earth herself, I tell you,
Earth herself. I whisper
because I'm ashamed. Isn't the earth our mother?
Isn't it we who've brought
this terror upon her?

A year before, this desert
had raised its claws to me,
importunate and indifferent, half-naked beggar
displaying sores at the city gates.
Now again, in the raw glare
of Lent. Spikes, thorns, spines.
Where was the beauty others perceived?
I could not.
        But when the Shoshone elder spoke,
last year and now once more,
slowly I began to see what I saw as ugly were marks
of torture. When he was young this was desert, too,
but of different aspect, austere but joyful.
A people's reverence illumined stony ground.
Now, as my mind knew but imagination strained to
                          acknowledge,
deep, deep and narrow the holes were bored
into the land's innards, and there, in savage routine,
Hiroshima blasts exploded, exploded, rape
repeated month after month for years.
What repelled me here was no common aridity
unappealing to lovers of lakes and trees,
but anguish, lineaments drab with anguish. This terrain

turned to the human world a gaze
of scorn, victim to tormentor.
                              Slowly,
revulsion unstiffened itself, I learned
almost to love
the dry and hostile earth, its dusty growth
of low harsh plants, sparse in unceasing wind;
could almost have bent
to kiss that leper face.

Uranium, with which we know
only how to destroy,

lies always under
the most sacred lands—

Australia, Africa, America,
wherever it's found is found an oppressed
ancient people who knew
long before white men found and named it
that there under their feet

under rock, under mountain, deeper
than deepest watersprings, under
the vast deserts familiar
inch by inch to their children

lay a great power.
                    And they knew the folly
of wresting, wrestling, ravaging from the earth
that which it kept
                    so guarded.

Now, now, now at this instant,
men are gouging lumps of that power, that presence,

out of the tortured planet the ancients
say is our mother.
                    Breaking the doors
of her sanctum, tearing the secret
out of her flesh.

But left to lie, its metaphysical weight
might in a million years have proved
benign, its true force being to be
a clue to righteousness —

showing forth
the human power
not to kill, to choose
not to kill: to transcend
the dull force of our weight and will;

that known profound presence, *un*touched,
the sign
providing witness,
            occasion,
            ritual
for the continuing act of
*non*violence, of passionate
reverence, active love.

If from Space not only sapphire continents,
swirling oceans, were visible, but the wars—
like bonfires, wildfires, forest conflagrations,
flame and smoky smoulder—the Earth would seem
a bitter pomander ball bristling with poison cloves.
And each war fuelled with weapons: it should be visible
that great sums of money have been exchanged,
great profits made, workers gainfully employed
to construct destruction, national economies distorted
so that these fires, these wars, may burn
and consume the joy of this one planet
which, seen from outside its transparent tender shell,
is so serene, so fortunate, with its water, air
and myriad forms of 'life that wants to live.'
It should be visible that this bluegreen globe
suffers a canker which is devouring it.

Cloudy luminous rose-mallow sundown,

                            suffusing the whole

roof-and-branch-interrupted lofty
air, blue fishscale slates,
wires, poles, trolleycars, flash
of window,
rectangular Catholic tall campanile abstracted
above North Cambridge, people heads down
leaving the store with groceries, bathed—
all! —utterly

            in this deepening, poised,

               fading-to-ivory oxbowed river of

light,
one drop
of crimson lake to a brimming
floodwater chalice
and we at the lees of it—ah,
no need to float, to long
to float upward, into it, sky itself
is floating us into the dusk, we are motes
of gold brushed from the fur
of mothwings, night is
breathing
close to us,
dark, soft.

Are they birds or butterflies?
They are sailing, two, not a flock,
more silver-white than the high
clouds, blissful
solitary lovers in infinite azure.

Below them, within the reef,
green shallows, transparent.

                       Beyond,
bounded by angry lace that
flails the coral,

          the vast,
ironic dark Pacific.

Tonga, 1979

Furry blond wheatfield in
predawn light — I
thought it was a frozen pond.

.

Small town, early morning.
No cars. Sunlit
children wait for the green light.

.

A deer! It leapt the fence,
scared of the train!
Did anyone else see it?

And twenty miles later
again a deer,
the exact same arc of gold!

.

After the trumpets, the
kettledrums, the
bold crescendo of mountains —

prairie subtleties, verbs
declined in gray,
green tones sustained, vast plainsong.

The Cabbage Field

Both Taine and the inland English child
were mocked for their independent
comparison of the sea to a field of cabbages:

but does this field
of blue and green and purple curling
turmoil of ordered curves, reaching

out to the smoky twilight's immense
ambiguousness we call
horizon, resemble

anything but the sea?

Each day's terror, almost
a form of boredom—madmen
at the wheel and
stepping on the gas and
the brakes no good—
and each day one,
sometimes two, morning-glories,
faultless, blue, blue sometimes
flecked with magenta, each
lit from within with
the first sunlight.

Between road and sidewalk, the broadleafed ivy,
unloved, dusty, littered, sanctuary of rats,
gets on with its life. New leaves shine gaily
among dogged older ones
that have lost their polish.
It does not require appreciation. The foliage
conceals a brown tangle of stems
thick as a mangrove swamp; the roots
are spread tenaciously. Unwatered
throughout the long droughts, it simply
grips the dry ground by the scruff of the neck.

I am not its steward.
If we are siblings, and I
my brother's keeper therefore,
the relation is reciprocal. The ivy
meets its obligation by pure
undoubtable being.

Tufts of brassy henna in the palm's
shaggy topknot—O Palm,
I like it, I like it!
                            And the dingy underlayer,
bedraggled skirt, tattered collar
around your furrowed neck, or is it your body,
that stout column?
                        You stay awake
all night every night
and tonight will be full moon. It's March,
and the ground beneath you
crunches under bicycle tires
where you littered it with your fruit,
those shiny brown things—I must take
a nutcracker to one some day, are they edible?
You let them fall
like a kid in the movies dropping a trail of popcorn.
                            Are you asleep up there,
your tousled green uncombed,
sunning yourself? Your way of paying
no attention, feline, and yet
strutting your crazy finery fit to kill,
I like it, I like it.

Come into animal presence.
No man is so guileless as
the serpent. The lonely white
rabbit on the roof is a star
twitching its ears at the rain.
The llama intricately
folding its hind legs to be seated
not disdains but mildly
disregards human approval.
What joy when the insouciant
armadillo glances at us and doesn't
quicken his trotting
across the track into the palm brush.

What is this joy? That no animal
falters, but knows what it must do?
That the snake has no blemish,
that the rabbit inspects his strange surroundings
in white star-silence? The llama
rests in dignity, the armadillo
has some intention to pursue in the palm-forest.
Those who were sacred have remained so,
holiness does not dissolve, it is a presence
of bronze, only the sight that saw it
faltered and turned from it.
An old joy returns in holy presence.

Their high pitched baying
as if in prayer's unison

remote, undistracted, given over
utterly to belief,

the skein of geese
voyages south,
                    hierarchic arrow of its convergence toward
                    the point of grace
swinging and rippling, ribbon tail
of a kite, loftily

over lakes where they have not
elected to rest,

over men who suppose
earth is man's, over golden earth

preparing itself
for night and winter.
                    We humans
are smaller than they, and crawl
unnoticed,

about and about the smoky map.

The Life Around Us

for David Mitchell and David Hass

Poplar and oak awake
all night. And through
all weathers of the days of the year.
There is a consciousness
undefined.
Yesterday's twilight, August
almost over, lasted, slowly changing,
until daybreak. Human sounds
were shut behind curtains.
No human saw the night in this garden,
sliding blue into morning.
Only the sightless trees,
without braincells, lived it
and wholly knew it.

O, the great sky!

Green and steep
the solid waves of the land,
breasts, shoulders, haunches,
serene.

The waveless ocean
arches its vertical silver,
molten, translucent.

Fine rain
browses the valley, moves
inland.
And flocks
of sunlight fly
from hill to hill.
The land
smiles in its sleep.

But listen . . .

no crisp susurration of crickets.
One lone frog. One lone

faraway whippoorwill. Absence.
No hum, no whirr.
And look:

the tigerish thistles, bold
yesterday,
curl in sick yellowing.

Drop the wild lettuce!
Try not to breathe!

Laboriously
the spraytruck
has ground its way
this way.
Hear your own steps
in violent silence.

In California: Morning, Evening, Late January

Pale, then enkindled,
light
advancing,
emblazoning
summits of palm and pine,

the dew
lingering,
scripture of
scintillas.

Soon the roar
of mowers
cropping the already short
grass of lawns,

men with long-nozzled
cylinders of pesticide
poking at weeds,
at moss in cracks of cement,

and louder roar
of helicopters off to spray

vineyards where *braceros* try
to hold their breath,

and in the distance, bulldozers, excavators,
babel of destructive construction.

Banded by deep
oakshadow, airy
shadow of eucalyptus,

miner's lettuce,
tender, untasted,
and other grass, unmown,
luxuriant,
no green more brilliant.

Fragile paradise.

    •   •   •   •

At day's end the whole sky,
vast, unstinting, flooded with transparent
mauve,
tint of wisteria,
cloudless
over the malls, the industrial parks,

the homes with the lights going on,
the homeless arranging their bundles.

. . . .

Who can utter
the poignance of all that is constantly
threatened, invaded, expended

and constantly
nevertheless
persists in beauty,

tranquil as this young moon
just risen and slowly
drinking light
from the vanished sun.

Who can utter
the praise of such generosity
or the shame?

So much is happening above the overcast!
Cloud poets, metaphysicians, essayists,
fabulists of the troposphere,
all at work, the material
their own metamorphic substance:
here a frank exposition, suds you could wash your clothes in,
there an abstract brocade that loops and swivels
in rivers of air. We glide low
across a forest, league on league
of trees in abundant leaf,
but white, silver-white, smudged with blue, tinged
with pink, like peonies—an entire summer
conjured in milky vapor, smoke of alabaster, slivers
of pearl. League on league
to a horizon more remote
than earth's horizons. Fading now,
curling, unfolding, imperceptibly flowing,
the blush paling. Dense thickets migrate
slowly across the fertile cloud-savannah, browsing.
And far aloft, in the sky's own sky, reclined,
the shepherd moon, propped on one elbow, watches
the flocks of drowsy cloud-lambs nibble their way out of being:
for darkness, even here, is gathering; the lunar gaze
dilates and begins to gleam,

while our enormous air-bus, throbbing west and south,
seems to tarry, fleck of metallic dust,
in this firmament where dreamy energies
sculpt themselves and winnow
epic epiphanies.

Nonchalant clouds below me
dangle shadows
into the curved river at Saskatoon.

Atlas of frontiers long-redrawn,
gazeteer of obsolete cities—
a jet-vapor garland
                    stretches and stretches to link
your incantations,
and breaks.
Still audible, stiffly revolving,
the globe of the world
creaks out enticements.
Decades pile up like thunderheads.
O Geography!
                    On your thick syrups
I float and float,
I glide through your brew
of bitter herbs.

Múmbulla Mountain,
low and round,
hums in green and hums

in tune, down in the Dreamtime.
World, you grow vaster. Our
time cannot
encompass you.

Composed by nature, time, human art,
an earthly paradise. A haze that is not smog
gentles the light. Mountains delicately frosted,
timbered autumnal hillsides copper and bronze.
Black-green of pine, gray-green of olive.
Nothing is missing. Ferries' long wakes pattern the water,
send to still shores a minor music of waves.
Dark perpendiculars
of cypress, grouped or single, cross immemorial
horizontals of terraced slopes, the outstretched wings,
creamy yellow, of villas more elegant
in slight disrepair than anything spick and span
ever could be. And all perceived
not through our own crude gaze alone but by the accretion
of others' vision—language, paint, memory transmitted.
Here, just now, the malady
we know the earth endures seems in remission—
or *we* are, from that knowledge that gnaws at us.
But only seems. Down by the lake the sign:
"Swim at your own risk. The lake is polluted."
Not badly, someone says, blithely irrelevant.
We can avoid looking that way,

if we choose. That's at our own risk.
Deep underneath remission's fragile peace,
the misshaped cells remain.

Lago di Como, 1989

Everything is threatened, but meanwhile
everything presents itself:
the trees, that day and night
steadily stand there, amassing
lifetimes and moss, the bushes
eager with buds sharp as green
pencil-points. Bark of cedar,
brown braids, bark of fir, deep-creviced,
winter sunlight favoring
here a sapling, there an ancient snag,
ferns, lichen. And the lake
always ready to change its skin
to match the sky's least inflection.
Everything answers the rollcall,
and even, as is the custom,
speaks for those that are gone.
—Clearly, beyond sound:
that revolutionary *'Presente!'*

Zones of flickering
                    water-diamonds
converse with almost-still
      glint of leaves along the poplar-row.

A dispersed array of water-birds relaxes
       afloat in autumn light,
one or another sometimes
                 diving casually.

                 And far across
         near the other shore,
    the lake is wearing a narrow, trembling
  band of silver,
a silver barely tinged with gold,
delicate tarnish.

        Someone's tapedeck booms and yells
        crescendo . . .
        pulses by and zooms
        out of the park.

        And quiet resumes,
        holding off as best it can
        peripheral sounds of human action —
        planes, subliminal traffic,

        (only one motorboat yet,
        it's a workday morning)—

        but admits
     the long and distant old-time wail of a train:
this quiet, this autumn sun,
          cool air and pale
          diaphanous light,
are generous.

Almost too late to walk in the woods, but I did,
anyway. And stepping aside for a moment
from the shadowy path to enter
darker shadow, a favorite circle of fir trees,
received a gift from the dusk:

a small owl, not affrighted, merely
moving deliberately
to a branch a few feet
further from me, looked
full at me — a long regard,
steady, acknowledging, unbiased.

Tired and hungry, late in the day, impelled
to leave the house and search for what
might lift me back to what I had fallen away from,
I stood by the shore waiting.
I had walked in the silent woods:
the trees withdrew into their secrets.
Dusk was smoothing breadths of silk
over the lake, watery amethyst fading to gray.
Ducks were clustered in sleeping companies
afloat on their element as I was not
on mine. I turned homeward, unsatisfied.
But after a few steps, I paused, impelled again
to linger, to look North before nightfall—the expanse
of calm, of calming water, last wafts
of rose in the few high clouds.
And was rewarded:
the heron, unseen for weeks, came flying
widewinged toward me, settled
just offshore on his post,
took up his vigil.
                    If you ask
why this cleared a fog from my spirit,
I have no answer.

The woods which give me their silence,
their ancient Douglas firs and red cedars, their ferns,
are not the wilderness. They're contained
in the two-mile circumference of an almost-island,
a park in city limits. Pleasure-boats crowd at weekends
into the small bay. The veils hiding the mountain
are not always natural cloud. Eagle and heron
speak of solitude, but when you emerge from forest shade
the downtown skyline rears up, phantasmagoric but near,
across the water. Yet the woods, the lake,
the great-winged birds, the vast mountain at the horizon,
are Nature: metonymy of the spirit's understanding
knows them to be a concentrate
of all Thoreau or Wordsworth knew by that word,
Nature: 'a never-failing principle
of joy and purest passion.' Thoreau's own pond
was bounded by the railroad, punctuated
by the 'telegraph trees' and their Aeolian wires.
All of my dread and all of my longing hope that Earth
may outwit the huge stupidity of its humans,
can find their signs and portents here, their recapitulations
of joy and awe. This fine, incised two inches
of goldsmith-work just drifted down, can speak

as well for *tree* as a thousand forest acres,
and tree means depth of roots, uprisen height, outreaching
branches.
This musical speech of wavelets jounced against reeds
as a boat's wake tardily reaches the shore,
is *voice of the waters*, voice of all the blue
encircling the terrestrial globe
which as a child I loved to spin
slowly upon its creaking axis — blue globe
we have seen now, round, small as an apple,
afloat in the wilderness we name
so casually, as if we knew it
or ever could know it, 'Space.'

That it is wide,
and still—yet subtly
stirring; wide and
level, reflecting the intangible sky's
vaster breadth in its own
fresh, cold, serene
surface we can
touch, enter, taste.
That it is wide
and uninterrupted save by
here a sail, there
a constellation of waterfowl—
a meadow of water
you could say,
a clearing amid the entangled
forest of forms and voices,
anxious intentions, urgent
memories: a deep, clear
breath to fill
the soul, an internal
gesture, arms
flung wide to echo
that mute
generous outstretching
we call *lake*.

They are going to
         daylight a river here—
that's what they call it, noun to verb.
A stream turned out
         years ago from its channel
to run in cement tunnels, dank and airless
         till it joined a sewer,
will be released—to sun, rain, pebbles, mud,
         yellow iris, the sky above it
and trees leaning over to be reflected!

At night, stars or at least streetlamps
         will gleam in it,
fish and waterbugs swim again in its ripples;
         and though its course,
more or less the old one it followed before its
         years of humiliation,
will pass near shops and the parking lot's
         glittering metallic desert, yet
this unhoped-for pardon will once more permit
         the stream to offer itself at last
to the lake, the lake will accept it, take it
         into itself,
the stream restored will become pure lake.

The fire in leaf and grass
so green it seems
each summer the last summer.

The wind blowing, the leaves
shivering in the sun,
each day the last day.

A red salamander
so cold and so
easy to catch, dreamily

moves his delicate feet
and long tail. I hold
my hand open for him to go,

Each minute the last minute.

I was welcomed here — clear gold
of late summer, of opening autumn,
the dawn eagle sunning himself on the highest tree,
the mountain revealing itself unclouded, its snow
tinted apricot as it looked west,
tolerant, in its steadfastness, of the restless sun
forever rising and setting.
               Now I am given
a taste of the grey foretold by all and sundry,
a grey both heavy and chill. I've boasted I would not care,
I'm London-born. And I won't. I'll dig in,
into my days, having come here to live, not to visit.
Grey is the price
of neighboring with eagles, of knowing
a mountain's vast presence, seen or unseen.

The mountain comes and goes
on the horizon,

> a rhythm elusive as that of a sea-wave
> higher than all the rest, riding to shore
> flying its silver banners—

you count to seven, but no,
its measure
> slips by you with each recurrence.

The mountain absent,
a remote folk-memory.

The peninsula
vanished, hill, trees—
gone, shoreline
a rumour.

And we equate
God with these absences—
Deus absconditus.
But God

is imaged
as well or better
in the white stillness

resting everywhere,

giving to all things
an hour of Sabbath,

no leaf stirring,
the hidden places

tranquil in solitude.

Today the mountain
is cloud,
pale cone of shadow
veiled by a paler scrim—

majestic presence become
one cloud among others,
humble vapor,
barely discernible,

like the archangel walking
with Tobias on dusty roads.

Though the mountain's the same warm-tinted ivory
as the clouds (as if a red ground had been laid beneath
not quite translucent white) and though the clouds
disguise its shoulders, and rise tall to left and right,
and soften the pale summit with mist,

                               yet one perceives
the massive presence, obdurate, unconcerned
among those filmy guardians.

The mountain
a moonflower in late
blue afternoon.

The bus
grinds and growls.
At each stop

someone gets off,
the workday over,
heads for home.

Trees in their first
abundance of green
hold their breath,

the sky is
so quiet, cloudless.
The mountain

mutely
by arcane power
summons the moon.

All day the mountain boldly
displayed its white splendor,
disavowing all ambiguity,

but now, the long June day
just closing, the pale sky
still blue, the risen moon
well aloft, the mountain
retreats from so much pomp,
such flagrant and superficial pride,

and drifts above the horizon,
ghostly, irresolute, more akin
to a frail white moth

than to the massive tension
of rock, its own bones, beneath
its flesh of snow.

Animal mountain,
some of your snows are melting,
dark streaks reveal
your clefts, your secret creases.
The light quivers,
is it blue, is it gold?
I feel your breath
over the distance,
you are panting, the sun
gives you no respite.

To be discerned
        only by those
                alert to likelihood —

the mountain's form
           beneath the milky radiance
                      which revokes it.

It lingers —
        a draft
           the artist may return to.

Ethereal mountain,
snowwhite foam hovering
far above blue, cloudy ridges—
can one believe you are not a mirage?

White as cloud above
a less-white band of cloud
the mountain
stands clear on a sky of
palest blue,
no other clouds in all
the sunny arch
of summer's last holiday.
And the mountain's
deep clefts and hollows,
the shadowy crevasses,
are that same
palest blue, as if
snow and rock,
the whole great mass of mountain,
were transparent
and one could look
through at more sky
southward.
Luminous mountain,
real, unreal sky.

Today the white mist that is weather
is mixed with the sallow tint
of the mist that is smog.
And from it, through it, breathes
a vast whisper:
the mountain.

Perhaps one day I shall let myself
approach the mountain—
hear the streams which must flow down it,
lie in a flowering meadow, even
touch my hand to the snow.
Perhaps not. I have no longing to do so.
I have visited other mountain heights.
This one is not, I think, to be known
by close scrutiny, by touch of foot or hand
or entire outstretched body; not by any
familiarity of behavior, any acquaintance
with its geology or the scarring roads
humans have carved in its flanks.
This mountain's power
lies in the open secret of its remote
apparition, silvery low-relief
coming and going moonlike at the horizon,
always loftier, lonelier, than I ever remember.

Sometimes the mountain
is hidden from me in veils
of cloud, sometimes
I am hidden from the mountain
in veils of inattention, apathy, fatigue,
when I forget or refuse to go
down to the shore or a few yards
up the road, on a clear day,
to reconfirm
that witnessing presence.

When my friend drove up the mountain
it changed itself into a big
lump of land with lots of snow on it
and slopes of arid scree.
Another friend climbed it the hard way:
exciting to stay the course, get to the top—
but no sense of height there, nothing to see but
generic mist and snow.
As for me,
when my photos come back developed,
there's just the lake, the south shore of the lake,
the middle distance. No mountain.
                How clearly it speaks! *Respect, perspective,
privacy,* it teaches. *Indulgence
of curiosity increases
ignorance of the essential.*
What does it serve to insist
on knowing more than that a mountain,
forbearing—so far—from volcanic rage,
blesses the city it is poised above, angelic guardian
at rest on sustaining air; and that its vanishings
are needful, as silence is to music?

The gleam of thy drenched
floors of leaf-layers! Fragrance
of death and change!
                 If there is only
now to live, I'll live
the hour till doomstroke
crouched with the russet toad,
my huge human size
no more account than a bough fallen:

not upward,
searching for branch-hidden sky:
I'll look
down into paradise.

Thy moss gardens, the deep
constellations of green, the striate
rock furred with emerald,
inscribed with gold lichen,
with scarlet!
             Thy smooth
acorns in roughsurfaced
precise cups!
             Thy black
horns of plenty!

Short grass, electric green, the ground
soggy from winter rain, Chaucerian
eyes of day, minute petals rose-tinted,
nourished by droppings of ducks and geese.
Hold fast what seem ephemera—
plain details that rise clear
beyond the fog of half-thoughts,
that rustling static, empty of metaphor.
Nothing much, or everything; all depends
on how you regard it.
                    On *if* you regard it.
                              Note the chalk—
yellow of hazel catkins, how in the wet
mild wind they swing toward spring.

We live our lives of human passions,
cruelties, dreams, concepts,
crimes and the exercise of virtue
in and beside a world devoid
of our preoccupations, free
from apprehension—though affected,
certainly, by our actions. A world
parallel to our own though overlapping.
We call it 'Nature'; only reluctantly
admitting ourselves to be 'Nature' too.
Whenever we lose track of our own obsessions,
our self-concerns, because we drift for a minute,
an hour even, of pure (almost pure)
response to that insouciant life:
cloud, bird, fox, the flow of light, the dancing
pilgrimage of water, vast stillness
of spellbound ephemerae on a lit windowpane,
animal voices, mineral hum, wind
conversing with rain, ocean with rock, stuttering
of fire to coal—then something tethered
in us, hobbled like a donkey on its patch
of gnawed grass and thistles, breaks free.
No one discovers

just where we've been, when we're caught up again
into our own sphere (where we must
return, indeed, to evolve our destinies)
—but we have changed, a little.

Notes

"Those Who Want Out," page 9: " . . . that the earth is an inert lump of matter, that our relationship to it is merely utilitarian, even that we might find a paradise outside it in space colonies. Such monstrous aberrations of thought are symptoms of the enchantment which blinds us to reality." —John Michell, *The Earth Spirit: Its Ways, Shrines & Mysteries* (Avon Books, New York 1975)

"It Should Be Visible," page 25: The allusion is to Schweitzer's phrase: "I am life that wants to live, among other lives that want to live."